TULE REVIEW
WINTER 2012

SPC
SACRAMENTO
POETRY CENTER

TULE REVIEW
WINTER 2012

Editors
Theresa McCourt and Linda Collins

Graphic Designer
Laura Martin

Cover Artist
Jane Blue

Special Thanks to the Following
The Albert and Elaine Borchard Foundation
The Estate of Anatole Lubovich
The Sacramento Metropolitan Arts Commission

Published by Sacramento Poetry Center Press
Sacramento Poetry Center
1719 25th Street
Sacramento, CA 95816
Ph: 916-979-9706
www.sacramentopoetrycenter.org

Published by
Sacramento Poetry Center,
a not-for-profit,
tax-exempt organization
registered in the state of
California. Contributions
to the review and the
organization are welcome
and tax-deductible.

ISBN-10: 098313622X
ISBN-13: 978-0-9831362-2-4

Cover Art Details
Photographer: Jane Blue
Title: Asilomar, 2008

Contents

Sacramento Poetry Center

Michael Duffett

DUST
  - from a diptych

The Door Ajar

"This jar shall be the prize to the dancer
Who dances more gaily than all others"
Is the oldest Greek inscription, the answer
To that conundrum that so often smothers
Thought: what is it that will last? What is it
That after all mundane things have gone, have passed
From memory, the future will visit
To know that what we once had been has cast
A shadow that the setting sun has left
Despite the laws of physics and of time?
What will future generations make of us?
Will it be that all we've done has been bereft
Of meaning? Is all life a wordless mime?
Can we discern the dancer's movements in the dust?

THE HEART LOVES
TO BE WARMED

Judith Tannenbaum

The Heart Loves to be Warmed

Waiting outside her own heart
For the door in the muscle to open.
Little blue door.
Three panes of glass in a row at the top
Where sunlight falls through.
For the heart loves to be warmed.

Right now, as I say, she is waiting.
Like a monk at the monastery gate
Whose hands rest against
His empty belly
As he sits day night day night
To prove a steady intention.
Expecting nothing but hoping
That gate will open and allow his bare feet
To cross – one then the other – over the threshold
Where the rest of his life will begin.
As it would have wherever he was.

Tim Sandefur

Marie

She is not ready to yield to his romance.
        Yes, she feels his fingers
        Brushing her pale temples
        Gingerly at night,
        Or squeezing too firmly her own;
        Hears his hoarse kiss when she wakes,
And watches his deepening caress in the mirror.
        But politely she declines
        When he offers her a ride,
        And patiently walks up the hill,
        Groceries stretching her back,
        Knowing that he waits at the top,
Patiently twirling that flower in his hands.
        She has a right to each step,
        And insists on having them all.
        A gentleman wouldn't complain.
        So, if you please, she will climb;
        So she will take her time.

Anne Babson

TRIBULATION LYRIC #2

The procedure:
Ly spy you un-
Paint, and your true
Mysterious
And you might be
For the other side
Think you were a
Its crumbs in some
Cease fire now. Loose
Grip. Lie down flat,
Too tired to fight,
Lullaby. If
Melody or
The lyrics, then we
Were raised by a
Not one of their
IV-Dripping
Identify
Cinnamon or
If you find a
Explosion of
Your teeth, you are
Issued but are
And fearfully

Since I can't real-
Der all that war
Intentions are
Even to yourself,
Interloping
And not even
Mole, carrying
Fold of your skin,
That thing in your
And when we grow
I'll sing you a
You recognize the
One or two of
Will both know you
Human alto,
Mechanical
Kindergartens.
scents of warming
Vanilla bean.
Horror at the sour
A lemon wedge in
Not factory-
Wonderfully
made.

Ann Wehrman

Bound

walking away from you
my ribs spread
cavern opens
heartbeat steady
somehow loyal to life
legs pump
foot leads foot
yet my steps slow
walking into a great wind
pulled back
by the caramel
ribbon of love
between us
heart to heart
no need to see it
eviscerate my inner self
love, emotion,
passion to the
base of my spine
pulls me back to you
pulls you to me
as I keep walking
away from you

Kiik A.K.

the season of pears and marmalade

Earlier today I was watching this guy
Ask three of his pals around him
Would anyone join him for a potpie

Something about their formality made it immensely
Pitiful to watch them dodge his invitation
Two gave excuses – a phone interview, a sick dog at home
The third just shrugged his shoulders and walked away

He really did not want to eat alone this guy
But so little hunger existed at that moment
I thought how sad it must be to eat a potpie by oneself!

It seemed I'd done it innumerable times before
But something had changed –
How tragic, how unfashionable it had recently become

In hell we starve! In heaven we feed each other!
And on earth we tirelessly pursue a companion –
In life or in potpie, I couldn't deny kinship with him

The reason I chose to write in this café was
I'd run into you twice before buying some pears and marmalade
And I wanted to run into you more

I kept hoping the season for pears and marmalade would return
O pear! You little god of grit and honey! O marmalade!
Savior of morning toast, kissing me stickily on my car ride to work

How difficult it is to get much serious writing done in this place!
Where I play conjurer, align my pen toward
The wondrous jar of preserves and doing all I can to compliment it –

The honey fired and whipped into amber
Shock of pome and pectin
Bitter suspension of citrus oil

And the constellation of zest and peel sailing through it –
Using my powers to summon your sweet tooth to return

Hoping once you're here your car will have run out of gas
Or your tires happily ruined in some gentle accident

O in hell today the pear went extinct
All the bees dropped dead

On earth no such luck – I grew fat
In my warm corner of this café

And in heaven your tow truck still hasn't arrived
And we will wait for it here together

*The quote "In hell we starve! In heaven we feed each other!" used in
this poem came from Jonathan Safran Foer's book "Extremely Loud
& Incredibly Close"*

Elizabeth Boskey

Size Queen

What really impresses me about a man
Is the size
Of his vocabulary.

The long, sibilant syllables
Which fall from his tongue
Stimulate the warm, secret places
Between my ears
And also somewhat lower.

A full bookshelf
Stuffed tight with language
Ideas and idiosyncrasies
To be swallowed by the eyes
Is a better aphrodisiac
Than any one designed
To be taken through the lips.

Alcohol may lower inhibitions
But words can open minds
Open hearts
Open thighs
And rarely leave a woman
Curled up on a cold floor
Wondering what she's done.

A passionate confession:
I'm a whore for words
Lascivious for language
A slut for stylistic prose.
The quickest way into my pants
         Is through my mind.

So in the service of base desire
There's one last thing I will admit
It's not just the size of a man's vocabulary
But how he uses it.

Kiik A.K.

love poem

Even if a hundred women volunteered
to take off their clothes

Dip themselves in milk
And roll around
On top of my cookies

I would not trade them for you
Rolling around
on my cookies

Or rolling around
asleep even
Rolling away from me

For you I would strip myself down
Squirt mustard across all my body
And rub myself against your sandwiches

There is no condiment I would not rub on myself for you
No marmalade or chutney I'd not endure
Swarming ants I wouldn't suffer

And no level of nakedness
I would not bare to you
At any hour
In your driveway
Where your family stood watching

Diana Thurm

Obsidian

i was taken aback by his smile
sparkling ivory against his indigo skin
obsidian
eyes of polished ebony
radiating light
like they could see a Sun beyond his Cimmerian world

is he sleeping tonight
under a sky the color of his skin
his onyx eyes gazing at those
white-hot points of light
burning holes in the sky
so he can peer at Heaven
the stars. his smile.
those onyx eyes.
no one who shines that bright should ever die.

JoAnn M. Anglin

He bought coffee, black

Take what you need, he said, his calloused palm
covered in coins — overlapping suns and moons —

seemed to cup silver promises, golden meaning.
His offered change offered a change that felt

like a listening ear, a hearth of heart, arms open.
I could see he had given before, could see him as

made for giving. His quizzical, patient smile held,
for a moment, a generous life, drew me to reach

out and choose. I wanted those coins in my mouth,
their warm metal taste of expectation.

April Peletta

Laundry

Breath caught on a fish hook,
dragging in air against the current of bright wet anxiety,
wet lumps cradled in my arms, soaking through my shirt,
pooling against flushed flesh.
Set the lumps on rusted iron table
standing in the need-to-be-mowed jungle grass.
Drag in air to my dry, pulsing lungs and wiggle the line,
testing the elasticity, durability,
wondering if it will hold the wet weight of our laundry.
This is the first time our clothes have sloshed together
in the spin cycle of my aged Whirlpool,
your plain boxers and my multi-patterned briefs swimming side by side.
Teeth gnaw at bottom lip as I untangle the wet mass of our lights,
divining if the line will hold, if the sun will gently
envelop them, or wring them dry and scratchy.
I release the line, pin our clothes together,
and walk away.

Maxima Kahn

Becoming Pearl

to love is pearl medicine
terrifying transformation
oozing grit and spit
unwinding to original aura

to love is unveiled garbage
poems in the furrows
a restless gypsy at the crossroads
earthward and earth bound

hardest homecoming
a house with the dirt still intact
i am covered in blood and shit
still beautiful unworthy

to love is to give up the ideal
find orchids in the muck
overcast freckled paradise
a ladder a painful door

you give me granite and agate
hard shine an eden where people eat
sleep fuck cry laugh
where we sharpen our pencils

to praise the ordinary
i resist it all
wanting evanescence
you give me the thick tang of reality

a cup filled with my own history
and evasions a choice
i'm rattling the bars of the cage
drink up you say drink up

A FEW THINGS I KNOW

Deborah J. Meltvedt

What we are made of

In dirt, we didn't grow things
but we dug, chucked earth
made swirled roads for toy trucks;
took out plastic zebras and gazelles
poured faucet water
down mounds of clay;
our own waterfalls –
made us yearn for Africa
just Mary Kay and me;
made us yearn for wildness & purpose,
for saving real things –
a thundered hoof,
the grace of fur flying
fresh dew on Kilimanjaro.

We found everything in dirt.
What better part of little girl-dom
than to squish the hell out of sugar
and spice and to fall half naked
into the open arms of your own backyard.
We were blonde hair spinning,
faces to heavens,
letting loose the sister circle
inhaling, gasping
see the butterfly swirl,
hear the dragonfly's wing.
Drown out the nighttime voices
release your hands from ears
there is a banquet of reprieve;
Winter still storms inside the house
but fog is lifting on the breezeway –

blue blinds the sky
sparrows spy the shadows
and Mud holds court for tiny hands.

Because we knew, as clear as sky
as painful as the bee sting;
that dirt receives us –
holds up the tiny backbones
lets loose the wavy hair.
And so we dug
past worms and twigs
waved arms to China
'till the earth was red, lovely, loosened;
'till we became the cells before conception
daughter atoms absorbed
and fell into the earth
hoping to materialize
past the honey and the spice
and into lovely bones that run and race,
into mouths that speak up,
into women –who, one day,
would become
more than the dirt.

Devi Sen Laskar

Aunt-by-Marriage

A few things I know about the ones
who came before you and paved the road
you now stand on: theirs was a blue world
tinged with stoicism and guilt.

Who came before you and paved the road
with unnamed humiliations, marriages,
tinged with stoicism and guilt
and children who glimmered immortality?

With unnamed humiliations, marriages,
as they played among the tall grass;
children who glimmered immortality:
they had mornings where there was nothing

as they played among the tall grass
to swallow their own yellowed anger.
They had mornings where there was nothing,
their faces masks of calm as they tended

to swallow their own yellowed anger –
manage the stove, the cradle, ruined men;
their faces masks of calm as they tended
to broken bottles, their tears, lost jewelry.

They managed the stove, the cradle, ruined men
you now stand on: theirs was a blue world
over broken bottles, their tears, lost jewelry –
a few things I know about the Ones.

Jenny Jiang

The Singer Slant-O-Matic Sewing Machine

Made of lumpy, dough-colored metal, it is heavy-ankled and
serious—like a woman with close-cut, unpainted fingernails,
broad and speckled with white. It's a factory of the fifties –
splendid with intention, the silver snaps of dials and gauges.
It is roped with thick brown electrical cords and the sweet
machine smell of oil, dust.

I see my mother, the soft hairs on her forehead lit in the glow
of the round yellow bulb. Before her, the bright needle and a
strand of blue thread tremble. The ball of her foot presses the
pedal, sets loose the single silver boot on its whirring, stamping
march. She flips levers, guides the cloth. Then snaps it out, rips
loose the thread with her teeth.

Before any seams, before pleats and darts, before the neat
slits for buttons, before the round dip of neckline—a woman
holds a length of muslin. She measures it against her bare,
outstretched arm. Now she can feel the pattern's crinkle of
umber tissue paper spreading under her fingers. She hears
the blade of her scissors crunching through the layers. She is
unafraid. She understands thread. She knows how to pull her
will and one idea, over and over, through the little slant of light
between foot and plate, needle and bobbin.

Lyn Lifshin

Girl Scout Camp

mostly, it was the smell of
pine on bunk beds girls
slept sideways on.
After the hike, scrambling
up rocks, my plump legs
less agile, less strong
than some others, I
plugged on, breathless,
wondering if I'd made it
to the top. Or if Mrs.
Sholes with her elephant
gray legs would glare.
There was no choice but
to go on. A few wild
flowers still on rocks, May
flowers and trillium,
yellow spotted adder's
tongue. If I was skinny as
Vivian or Regina, then
I'd move like a doe through
the branches. I was
still haunted by the way
I left camp at 8, half crazed
with homesickness. But
as the blaze of sun fell
behind the birches and oaks
and in the fire we roasted
marsh mellows in the
embers that leaped
and danced, I imagined
gypsies in the light.

Chocolate dripped on our
fingers sweetening the
night and the pine smell
grew thicker, a green
perfume that would
flavor dreams
and through the logs, the
moon, a vanilla saucer.

April Peletta

Firecrackers

Bombs of laughter explode
from lips on the back patio.
Stars sway from my mother's ears
as she serves margaritas and bowls of salad
to the circle of moms. Red, white, and blue sewn
into their clothes as they re-cross shaved legs,
suck ice and nicotine.

At the open flame barbeque
my father presses the spatula into ground beef.
He makes indentations like faded handprints
as the horseshoe of dads watches pink flesh
turn brown as the freckles on their wives' calves.

Beer bottles clutched tight
as the pigskins they used to throw,
the men holler at sons who play tackle on the grass.
slap their boys on sunburned backs,
let them sip brewskis.

Later dads teach daughters to look at the sun
through the bottoms of empty bottles,
but that makes the world brown,
so we wander away.

In unison we unfurl white beach towels across red brick
and one by one cannonball off the lip of the pool.
We break the blue bowl into a thousand clear shards,
our voices exploding into a wet nebula of muffled sound,
where the only things pulling us to the surface
are slashes of light cracking the sky.

Peggy Garrison

Big Ben

The glassy light of night,
Cuz and I wandering around Water Street
in high heels and short skirts
looking for a particular bar,
lights like pin-pricks
sparkle from the buildings bordering the river,
the river itself, quiet
and dark; we're on the edge
ready to board the bad ship Debauchery,
my ticket, a Seven and Seven ("a nice
drink for a lady" my father once said).
We enter the warm hold of the tavern
and one masquerade is exchanged for another;
as a life preserver virtue has all the strength
of a dunked doughnut; sin is the winner;
the bartender's suggestive banter,
the mirror's glow – I love it;
the mosquito crawling up my leg
feels like a feather.

Adrian C. Louis

Kisses: Lovelock, Nevada 1945

Studious by daylight, giddy &
tight-skirted under moonlight,
two rez girls cross the train tracks
& skip towards the skid row
of a small, desert town.

The roiling saloons & loud-ass
jukes give them goose-bumps.
They want in on the joyful cascade
of V-J Day & yearn to kiss any & all
the GIs headed home on Hwy. 40.
Gray buses on two-hour layovers
deploy scores of drunk soldiers.
My aunt kisses a swabby who says
he's only seen Indians in movies.
My mother kisses a sergeant who
was headed home to Albuquerque.
Deep inside her egg sac the eye
that will be I watches & waits.

WHAT'S LEFT

Jeffrey Alfier

Reclaiming the Abandoned House

It's been two decades since a neighbor's wife
bounced her screams off every wall in the place,
the husband tripping over his exit,
speechless, stoned and breathing brutal vapors
into primetime air, never looking back
as the kids watched their mother's Lucky Strike
twist smoke above them like a charmed cobra.

The way liquor bottles are strewn,
closets and carpets rifled with trespass,
dry wall and mirrors hollowed by fists,
this shack could've been a roadhouse, far south
of any man's meridian of hope.

Today, the scent of virgin two-by-fours
bathes the air sifting the renovations.
New doors lean against the front bay
window, awaiting their proper union
with hinges and hasps; plumbers, carpenters,
roofers, at work against looming weather,
rain making soft sounds on the uncut lawn,
untrimmed roses, and someone rushing past.

Tim Sandefur

Relics

I couldn't help but skim a fingertip
Across the line long frozen under varnish;
Stiff, beside a cabinet full of tarnished
Medals, the antique man with rueful lips

Said it was a German piece. "The repair
Was delicately made; perhaps some fight;
Voices clashed, severing the night;
The door was slammed; feet pounded down the stairs.

Careful fingers tried to smooth the rupture
Later; reattach the separate planes.
But no mend can realign the severed grain
Or knit again the patient tensile structure.

Time has sanded smooth this subtle crease,
Now overlooked. And yet no strength reclaimed
Is ever without seams. The wound remains,
Like every breach of nature's single peace."

Kenneth DiMaggio

Made in USA (Front Porch)

Nothing more
American than
this front porch
filled with girls
women and boys
no older than
eleven because
after that they just
start running with
Satan and it is only
when they are in
a coffin or prison
that their Grandmas
Moms and sisters
can claim them and so
these rotted steps and
kitchen knife carved
rails and posts will still
hold them in rockers
crates and pulled out car seats
another generation of
women trying not
to lose and then hoping
they can reclaim
and from more than just
coffins or prisons

Kenneth DiMaggio

Made in USA (Geography)

The law calls it
Grand Theft Auto
but your soul knows
that ever since folks
have been coming
here they've been stealing
somebody else's geography
which just gets
smaller and smaller
and for yours it's just
a town no bigger than
a 10-minute joyride
and a 7-to-15 stretch
in prison which still can't
stop a heart too big
wild & illegal just like
its country for which
only a crime or a theft
will let you imagine
yourself as more
than just a thief
or a criminal

John Aylesworth

Cars Without Hubcaps

Leave Wal Mart and start out Route 50
toward rusty double-wides and farms
left to forest, places where crossroads
had names once, stops on trails west.
Old Chevys and Fords with wrinkles
rattle away, leaving town for homesteads
tucked under hills claimed by pioneers
manifesting destiny, without hubcaps.
What's left is mud and gravel,
and folks with only names to cling to,
legacies lost when the four lane
cut through the valley, made tradition
and birthright as black as cars without hubcaps.

Emily Pérez

Hush

Let's just say I was asleep
and now I've risen.
I prefer that we don't call it death
but it's true, my life anchored
to a sunken ship, a woman bound
to a drowning man—is hardly living.

As for how I cut that rope,
let's just say I used a trick.
As for what they call me now,
let's just say it is not wife, help-
meet, or blessed-among women.

It's true that women do conform.
When poured into a vessel
occupied by mystery I was control.
With misery, I was contempt.

And now that I'm the keeper
of the cup I live in,
now my cup is empty?

Let's just say I am both squall
and harbor, the blaze
and air-tight room.

Let's just say that nothing
grazes in my sheets or greets me
by my hearth-side,
that absence
is my perfect groom.

Devi Sen Laskar

Shape Shifting

Since I was the unemployed poet who hadn't
published in eight years my husband
said I had to find an accountant to help us save
money. I wanted to write a sestina
and since there were five of us, I asked each one
for a word: Mine was collection.
He said spoil and the girls said present, rose, bend.
The accountant added close.
At first I thought I was writing about the migration
of monarchs, the milkweed pit-stops
between Vermont and the mountainous forests
where they're known to swarm whole
groves of pine and eucalyptus in central Mexico
before trekking back north to die.
But it was hard to find six different uses for fly
besides the obvious ones about sex
and flight and who needs to read another sestina
about endangered butterflies
whose stained-glass wings rival cathedral windows
in Europe? Cities I'd never see
again since my now ex-husband ran off with our
accountant and currently has custody
of the children while I have custody of the credit
card bills. Then I thought I'd use
the leftover material to fashion a sestina about fairy
tales and benevolent godmothers who rescue
distressed damsels the way
my lawyer refinishes distressed furniture
on weekends that other people have warped
by using the chair arms as coasters
for their espresso or chardonnay. But I got tired
of the repetition of distress

and I didn't want to write about my attorney's
obsession with other people's inability
to manage their own possessions and nobody
would read another rewrite
of Cinderella, however compelling the form.
Besides, fairy tales were for children
and I can't even see mine without written
permission from my ex-husband's new wife
who now knows every scintilla about me,
that mousy-haired, green-eyed, statuesque
accountant of marital discord. I wrote out by
hand my fractured phrases and disjointed
thoughts and took to them with a pair
of scissors, my black-inked scrawl now on long
strips of white paper; I unraveled a pile of wire
coat hangers my ex-husband would
no longer be using to hang up his double
breasted jackets and monogrammed silk
shirts and fashioned a mask of a face that didn't
rival a real artist's but I was pleased
with it and with the help of glue from the kids' art
caddy I made a literary mummy
face, words swirling between the bell-shaped
ears. Rose and bend on each eye, spoil
and present on the lips and collection just
at the chin. Close on the forehead. The whites
of the eyes were like egg whites surrounding
a poached egg and I was hungry
for the first time in months so I washed my
hands and hung up my new face on a nail
that used to hold up a picture of my ex-husband
and me and I went downstairs
and cooked breakfast and decided I would be
a unknown multimedia artist and give up
writing because who needs another poet in
the world, one who can't even write a sestina?

Geoff Stevens

Just the Two of Us

With love in its 30th week
we open our eyes and find
other people there
sharing our cinema
walking in our park
punting on our gondola

They are even interrupting
our loving glances
at the office
suggesting they visit us at home
walking unannounced into our conversations
inveigling themselves into our thoughts
invading our intimate bedtime dreams

These people are inconvenient
to our relationship
they spoil the simplicity and intensity
of our affair
Once we had only one emotion
now there are many
all our stifled complications are reborn

They have contaminated all that was pure between us
and we have no stronger drug available
than our infatuation
we have become weak
unable to combat the threats to our togetherness
can no longer fight the fact
that you slept with Rodney from Accounts
and I with Elsie from Customer Services

OUT OF REACH

Deborah J. Meltvedt

Doctor's Office

I grew up in the land of gynecology -
women waiting.
There is the push of heavy doors
into my father's practice.
We are dropped into the back room like shopping bags
to wait with Highlights magazines and obstetrical manuals,
eating Saltine crackers and drinking 7UP.
We play with the silliness of plastic wombs
finger fallopian tubes
think of drawing fat smiles
on the moose-head likeness of uterine anatomy charts.

In later years, we work in his office
in the kingdom of white coats -
women waiting.
Words like mittleschmertz, yeast infections, and
salpingoopherectomy
fall easily off our tongues.
We laugh at the woman on the other side of the phone
who claims her vibrator makes her pee;
And we look down, solemn eyed, when
the sound of the Doppler goes silent
against the bulge of a belly –
that ripened once, then shriveled.

Years later, I make my own appointments
in towns far from my father's reign.
And when my name is called,
I squeeze polite-lipped through a room of
sausage legs and swollen bodies
of women giving so much more of themselves away.

Years later, I kill time
lying against paper sheets,
bite my own tongue when the doctor
reaches for something soft beneath my soul –
learn to scoot down and shut up
to stare up at ceilings,
waiting.

Deborah J. Meltvedt

Miscarriage

In manila bed
it rests –
on the peeling kitchen shelf
wedged on the ledge
we access by the tallest of our tip toes
on sturdy, ugly chairs.

Here, she holds up Terminology:
endometrium; spontaneous abortion; blighted zygote
Out of reach
like the leftover lamb
held high on a plate
far from the begging dog
so tall on its hind legs
but not tall enough
to reach the shelf.

Elizabeth Boskey

Hope

I misplaced it
About the time
That the third friend
Who had always told me she hated children
Announced that she was having one

The box
Pandora kept it in
Was small and plain.
Made of bare, unstained wood,
Unremarkable, and easily missed
I would be unsurprised to learn
I had thrown it away
The last time I cleaned out the basement

I first noticed it was gone
The day my last unpaired friend from college
The one who had so often declared
Her unabashed disinterest in living with a man
Told me that she was engaged to be wed

In the weeks since I noticed its absence
I have shown an alarming tendency
To search inside other people's bags
Open locked doors
And rummage through trash bins
In search of a small, plain box
Made of battered, dented pine
Faded and brown

Holly Day

Denied

she only put up with the beatings
for the baby's sake, the baby she knew
he and she would have some day. dreams
of bright park days, tiny pink sunbonnets
first Christmases and school bus rides
sustained her through black nights
of broken dishes, flying fists
forgettable words.

when she found out she couldn't have her child
any child, ever, ever, it was all she could do
to keep breathing. all the wasted days.
all the secret saving, planning, praying,
bright dreams of beach days and
one big happy family
they would never be.

ARS POETICA

Sarah Heller

Ars Poetica

There are a few words I can never remember –
geranium, and the dog that looks like a wolf –
or is part wolf – a husky, I think.
And whenever I see a geranium,
I say, I can never remember the word for that plant.
It's my grandmother's, the one that
I took home on the ferry, with the green scented stems.

I shake out my head to evoke the word
like I'm shaking rain off my fur —
I'm the husky, trying to remember the name
for geranium. Or I'm the green plant breathing,
sensing the blue eyed dog —
or I'm here trying to break through to a poem,
through shifting windows, into fog.

Matthew Rodgers

The World Asked Me to Write a Pretty Poem and I Thought of the Color Crimson

The Darkness is as Gentle as that Dreamed About Place
the stars, the moon, celestial splendor
the sunset disappears under willow trees
and today the wind reminded me of fire
of skyscrapers, of beggars, of wealth,
the inspiration is red
the creativity is red
the romance is red
and the night is black
they are not the conquerors of the world
but the conquerors of time
these burning effigies
of moths that go towards the flame
snuffed out, but everlasting
and the sun, is on fire.

Tim Sandefur

I Don't Need a Myth for Poetry

I don't need a myth for poetry.
I just need a wave of tiny photons,
Born in seething plasma filaments
Blasted from the surfaces of suns
So far away they also seem to be
Countless tiny particles of light,
Racing at the speed of time through frigid
Folds of weird eternity until
A thousand generations later, Earth
Will weave them into veils, dancing,
Bending, delicate, in northern skies,

Or, ending their immeasurable journey,
Fall through the lensing sky to crash
In silence on the surfaces of leaves,
Igniting autumn's furious and silent
Burn; red and gold, they spin, and then
They fall in curling wind, and in the fields,
Once again they yield their energy.

Emily Pérez

Raveling Round the Lake

Raveling round the lake the path,
the pointlessness. A thought
refrained from blooming.

If a circle is a wish
I'm weary now with wishing,
the walkers on this shore

waste more than just a Sunday.
The light will take its long low bow
round afternoon, the geese will fill

with swimming, they'll fall
to preening in what trickles down
around among them:

a white so cold with wanting.
When ever did we give
up endings, trade them in

for middling, a muddling lean
and lingering? Tonight's more apricots
and longing, a yellow so red

an orange inflamed
with warming, oh, to swallow
all that waning sun.

Zara Raab

Towpaths

The day she went shuffling through the landfill
for odd treasures, pawing through old tires
beneath snowy tangles of wires,
she found a towpath among the jumble,
a path tamped by mules who long ago
worked the canal, pulling their cargos.

Further on, she found the rusty rails. These
she might have followed to the horizon,
the ties leading to derelict stations,
yet so orderly, sequential, it seemed trees
were stretching their long limbs out on the ground,
like the rungs of a ladder tipped down.

She tapped her way, spent entire years
following the freeway to the rivers,
crouching below the cities, cars rushing
like falls of water, light, quick crossings,
low-beamed, the travellers lost in their cars
accomplishing by instinct their swift arcs.

Beneath the cosmos' umbrella of stars,
she skirted the rain. While the sycamores
grew over the streets, she stirred potions
in measured, dreamy improvisation,
unfolding worlds of her own making,
with the help of the dead and the living.

Mark Wisniewski

Woman, You Know Who You Are

days ago the editor of a highly
regarded literary
magazine wasn't wearing a seatbelt
& hit a guardrail & expired rather
gruesomely & since then various writers have
commented publicly about how tough
& witty she was
how demanding of men when it came

to her rights how she disdained this
fellow & that but how she always used (yes
again) "wit"

& I keep saying nothing since she
never accepted my work
rejecting me brusquely
never with wit & as much as I hate
to say it
her responses to me placed her
among the souls I'd never choose
to hang with

still I am shocked by her
absence miffed at her for rejecting
that seatbelt & just for this moment grateful
to her yet

again for again
causing me to sigh
& shut up
& write

Luisa M. Giulianetti

Some Days

To see a World in grain of sand/ And Heaven in a Wild Flower/
Hold Infinity in the palm of your hand/And Eternity in an hour
—William Blake, Auguries of Innocence

Some days awaken
like an origami crane.
Each crease conjures the next.
The velvet motion of hours:
honeyed dawn to evening lull.

Some,
a desert storm—
electric orange
cracks, dirt-sizzle
before silence.
You search for a trace,
a pebbled trail,
but come up empty:
no atmospheric effect,
no burning bush or toppled tree,
to mark your ground.

Others fold into themselves,
a slur of minutes,
of hours.
You unhinge robotic limbs
and scan for creases
that allow sun.

Even on such days,
from an ordinary square,
from folding and unfolding,
pressing, twisting,
opens a bird,
thirsty for flight.

Mark Wisniewski

Polish Boy

sometimes in the middle
of a night I'll wake
& start wondering where they
came from: the words & conflicts &
oddities in all those
stories printed under the Polish
boy's name

this troubles
me into fearing my source
will dry up

leaving me as a kind of Joe
Namath of literature

hobbled
permanently

Broadway grin yellowed

stance irreparably
bent:

done

sometimes I'll then consider
my parents

the verbal flow my father's
side lent
the desire for goodness
that came from my mother & I'll think
that maybe I owe

it all to them & that if the spirits of their
ancestors – wherever they
are – decide to pull some
plug on me

I'll become forever
a disgrace

certainly a disappointment to all those
supposed friends on Facebook
& maybe

worst of all

an enemy
of myself

then I'll continue
to lie
still

that much closer
to daylight

IT SEEMED LIKE ANGELS

Heather Judy

Canto

Something between
feeling and felt.

She walked into the river. Pockets
rock-heavy. Heavy with madness, she
said. And she feared. She said she feared she
would not recover. They
had plans. How they would
kill themselves in the event
of an invasion.

And she felt herself
invaded.

It was a walking hour, a waking
hour. Time to rest with
movement. And so she took her
walk. She sat cross-legged in
the waiting place. Staring
at the clock. Large, mounted
high for everyone to see. Don't be
late. Don't wait here
too long, said the now
grinning now frowning face.

Somewhere in her, she felt
herself a native place.

His tick made her nervous. A twitch
of the mouth. And she swore
she heard his
muffled laugh. Stifling.

And the native
feeling felt.

She wrote many words.
She said she could not write.
She could not follow.

She began again.
She wrote the words.
She fingered the words.
She thumbed the obvious blue vein.

She said she
no longer felt.

She said to break the door
down. She couldn't get out
of her head. With so many others
to think of, so many voices
to hear. Listening. Telling. She
scratched and clawed
at words, trying to keep
up. Trying
to follow. Their clamor
for attention grew.
She said she could not
keep up. With so many others
to hear, she said she simply
could not.

Devi Sen Laskar

What Happens Next

"I know sirens are especially bad news when they come for you."
–Terrance Hayes

Everybody, and I mean everybody on the interstate
sitting through the aftermath of that forty-car pileup, replete
with helicopters and jaws of life, candy-red fire
engines and highway patrol clad in ash-colored uniforms
and giant holstered guns, heard them. At first, it sounded like bees
swarming just before the mind alerts you that bees hum in groups
when gunning for you, then it switched to a children's choir,
well, a choir from an all-girls school, girls who were still at a distance.
As it got closer, it seemed like angels but not the kind we think
of at Christmas; and closer still, the temperature skied high,
the ground trembled and even the trees on the other side of the sound
barriers swayed to this music; everyone got out of their cars
and the women looked up and saw feathered bodies looming
as the men all dropped to their knees and screamed. I thought at first
they were the furies but saw their childish faces, beauty
and terror, and knew they were the sirens coming for us all.

Holly Day

My Dog's Dreams

My dog tells me that our days are numbered
that any day now, the skies will open and dog angels
will flutter down to the earth, wave spears tipped with
lightning
and kill us all. Dogs
will inherit the earth.

I pat my dog's head, scratch him behind the ears
stare deep into those droopy brown eyes
look for signs of malice. He speaks of
the inevitable destruction of mankind
with the same fervent passion as he does
when requesting new chew toys
or announcing the approach of the mailman.

He says he wishes he could save me, but
the new world will belong only to dogs. He
asks me to pray with him
pray for a maybe world where I'll be saved
as some sort of dog slave, a pet.
He licks my hand with his soft, warm tongue.

Maxima Kahn

The Grieving and the Dying

The grieving and the dying
just go on and on. It's amazing
what a life they have,
this life of loss.

Neither right nor wrong,
this fucking heart.
Who knew the story
would be all about pain?

Who knew
you'd be asked
to give everything, then
give some more?

How is it that the birds
singing and chirping this morning
are so unconcerned by this,
do not even know

loss's name? How could humans
ever think they are better
than the animals, a life
of suffering superior to a life of song?

You'd do me a great kindness,
you gods, to let me come back
with flight and music as my only goals.
They are my only real goals now—

but I don't reach them
with the ease the birds do—
and then there's love—
that's the one, the hook

where I am caught and the flesh
around my mouth tears,
and I bite down harder,
unwilling to let go.

Michael Duffett

DUST
 - from a diptych

Life Almost Rhymes

The first place we stayed in California
Was called The Stardust Motel; it was on
Wilshire Boulevard in Los Angeles.
We now have an acre of land in the north,
I have a steadier job (in those days
I was an itinerant bookseller)
I now profess poetry at a college
And am able, at night, to write sonnets.
The one that precedes this blank verse I wrote
Before I heard a whining from the deck
Where we don't have a pool. The Stardust had,
And I have a photograph of it
Somewhere in my papers, with a view
Of the tawdry daytime neon sign
That gives the place its poetic name at night.
On our deck, thirty years later, our dog,
Half blind, overweight, had become stranded
At the bottom of the steps, too lame
To ascend under his own canine steam.
So I had to help him, stumble out barefoot
Into the night and lift him, grunting,
Both of us, to the back door of the bedroom.
As I did, I glanced up at the night sky,
Non-neon-lit, and had the following thought:
Is this the answer to the query
That my poem poses? Is this life's meaning:
Helping a lame dog ascend a stair in
Stardust at half past four in the morning?

Gordon Preston

"Jane"

is a short story by
Theresa Williams and
somewhat independent
of it there is a photograph
on the magazine page, a black
and white print
of a woman in
bare feet, a lady
somewhat blurred,
wearing a slip type
summer dress though
the grays in it give a
coolness look,
like after a rain or
one about to begin,
shedding a sadness
her walking away
from the camera,
from us, her backside,
beautiful shoulders and
hips absorbing light,
giving a fullness of
her leaving into the
wet path laid out
sway of her left
arm so complete
as everything
else in the
world right
now this
moment
seems so
utterly
unattainable.

Jenny Jiang

Look A Gift Horse in the Mouth

Peel back the lips' satin purse
and count every bent and yellowed coin.

Let the muscled tongue, green with hay spittle,
lick the salt sweat from your probing fingers.

Later, pitched across
a broken field of green and stone,

you lean over the steaming umber neck,
your thighs, damp and burning, grip the sides;

you pull lightly or urgently
on the leather ribbon of reins and

the steel rings against the teeth
like a clapped bell through

the blood-muscle-bone-tendon-horse
that turns or balks or continues its long throw.

Say I have received this.
At least know what can be known.

Each grooved cliff wears itself away
by the long practice of eating

the sun wrapped in a sheath of clover.
And all things are so.

The bank of oaks, heavy clouds, fragments of sky
slide past like water.

Listen now—
the sure faint throb

the hard lovely echo
of the body's red clock.

Michael Campagnoli

Long Shadows

Before dawn,
in mirrored light but no sun,
she saw the birds leaving.
Going south. Row upon row
in strict cuneal formation.
Or raucous, in cluttered disarray.
Flying low and fading high up in the sky.
Heading out.

Later, running past the cove
in mittens and hat,
she heard them cry far in the distance:
a nameless feeling of affection and regret.
Only the loons remained,

Old friends.
Their time would come, too.

The time of long shadows.

Mark Jackley

GAR
1900-1995

Jim Beam and a splash of water,
leave the bottle on the table.
I lived to be three hundred eighty-six in Red Sox years.

Ted Williams would uncoil on a fastball like a cobra,
but the summer sun would take
its sweet and silent time

creeping across the Fenway grass
on its way to here,
wherever that is. Look, it's back to zero-zero

on the Monster once again.
If you're keeping score, no one or everyone
has made it safely home.

Contributors

Jeffrey Alfier is a two-time Pushcart prize nominee and a nominee for the UK's Forward Prize for Poetry. His poems have appeared recently in *Vallum* (Canada) and *Post Road*, with work forthcoming in *New York Quarterly*. His latest chapbook is *Before the Troubadour Exits* (2011). His first full-length book of poems, *The Wolf Yearling*, will be published in 2012 by Pecan Grove Press. He serves as co-editor of *San Pedro River Review*.

JoAnn M. Anglin of Sacramento, CA, is a member of Los Escritores del Nuevo Sol (Writers of the New Sun) and the Writers' Circle. Besides a chapbook, *Words Like Knives, Like Feathers* (Rattlesnake Press), her work is in *The Sacramento Anthology: One Hundred Poems*, the *Anthology of the Third Sunday Poets, The Pagan Muse*, and in *Voces del Nuevo Sol*, as well as other regional publications.

Kiik Araki-Kawaguchi, also known as **Kiik A.K.**, is a graduate student of fiction at the creative writing program at University of California, San Diego. He previously earned an M.A. at University of California, Davis where his poetics thesis was entitled *The Joy of Human Sacrifice*. The poems *the season of pears and marmalade* and *love poem* were written for HMK.

John Aylesworth teaches handicapped kids in Southeastern Ohio. He earned an M.A. in Creative Writing and a PhD., in Comparative Arts from Ohio University. He lives in Athens with his wife, two dogs, and a cat named Lucy.

Anne Babson won the Columbia Journal Prize, the Artisan Journal contest, and was nominated for both 2001 and 2005 Pushcarts for work appearing in *The Haight Ashbury Literary Journal* and *Ilya's Honey*. Her work has recently appeared in *Bridges, Barrow Street, Connecticut Review, The Pikeville Review, Rio Grande Review, Atlanta Review*, and many other publications.

Elizabeth Boskey is a sexual health researcher and a prolific writer of non-fiction. She is currently working on a poetry collection about her personal demons. You can find out more information about her various pursuits at **www.elizabethboskey.com**

Michael Campagnoli's work has appeared in *New Letters, Nimrod, The Southern Humanities Review, Rattle, Natural Bridge, New York Stories, Saint Ann's Review, Quiddity*, and *Chiron Review*, among others. He won the New Letters Poetry Prize in 2002 and the All Nations Press Chapbook Award in 2004.

Holly Day is a housewife and mother of two living in Minneapolis, MN. Her poetry has recently appeared in *The Oxford American, The Midwest Quarterly*, and *Coal City Review*. She recently co-authored the book *Guitar All-in-One for Dummies* with guitarist Jim Peterik of the band Survivor, and just finished writing the second edition of *Music Theory for Dummies*.

Kenneth DiMaggio teaches Humanities at Capital Community College in Hartford, a city discarded but still dangerous like an old hypodermic. He has published his poetry in *The Outlaw Bible of American Poetry, Plainsongs, CC&D, Quercus Review*, and other publications. Darkling Publications will publish his chapbook *American Gothic*.

Michael Duffett's work has appeared in England, Japan, India, New Zealand, Hawaii, and California. He was born in London, educated at Cambridge, and has been a college professor, according to the publisher of his best-known book *Forever Avenue* (John Daniel, 1987) "on every continent except South America and Antarctica." He is currently Adjunct Associate Professor of Linguistics and Religion at Delta College in Stockton, CA.

Peggy Garrison earned her M.A. in creative writing from the City College of New York. She teaches creative writing workshops at New York University and is the author of *Ding the Bell*, a book of poems illustrated by Lesley Heathcote (Poetry New York, 1999). Her work has appeared in many publications including *The Literary Review, Beloit Fiction Journal, South Dakota Review*, and *Global City Review*.

Luisa M. Giulianetti, a Bay Area native, works at the University of California, Berkeley as an administrator and writing instructor. Her graduate work was in 20th Century American literature, with an emphasis in African American literature. She enjoys teaching and helping students develop their voices as writers. She is published in *The Owl* (currently the *Santa Clara Review*) and the *Lily Literary Review*.

Sarah Heller's work has appeared in *RealPoetik, Painted Bride Quarterly, Pembroke Magazine, NextBook, The Temple/El Templo, Lady Churchill's Rosebud Wristlet, Thin Air, The Apocalypse Anthology* (Flying Guilliotine Press), *Literary Companion to Shabbat* (NextBook Press), and *Hayloft*. She lives in Brooklyn, NY, and teaches Creative Writing at Rutgers University.

Mark Jackley is the author of several chapbooks, most recently *Every Green Word* (Finishing Line Press) and a full-length collection called *There Will Be Silence While You Wait* (Plain View Press). He lives in Sterling, VA.

Jenny Jiang has published in the online journal *Convergence* and the Sacramento Poetry Center's publication *Poetry Now.* Jiang has also won several awards, including the Grand Prize, at the Annual Berkeley Poets' Dinner. She writes extensively for Oak Hills Church where she, her husband, and her son serve and worship.

Heather Judy is a graduate of California State University, Sacramento and recently received her M.F.A. in Poetry from Mills College. Currently, she can be found climbing the trees near Berkeley, California.

Maxima Kahn is a writer of poetry, fiction, and essays. She teaches private workshops on poetry and the creative process, and has taught at the University of California, Davis Extension. Her poetry has appeared in *Eclipse, Meridian Anthology of Contemporary Poetry, Hardpan, Poem, Borderlands, Left Curve, Eureka Literary Magazine,* and elsewhere. She is also a violinist, a composer, and a dancer.

Devi Sen Laskar is a native of Chapel Hill, NC. She holds a B.A. in journalism and English from UNC-Chapel Hill, an M.A. in South Asian Studies from the University of Illinois, and an M.F.A. from Columbia University. Her poems have been published in *The Atlanta Review, Tule Review, The Squaw Valley Review, Pratichi,* and *The North American Review* in 2009 and 2011, where they were finalists for the James Hearst Prize.

Lyn Lifshin has edited four anthologies and written many books including her most recent, *All the Poets Who Have Touched Me, Living and Dead: All True, Especially the Lies* (World Parade Books). Her other books include *Ballroom* (March Street Press), *The Licorice Daughter: My Year With Ruffian* (Texas Review Press), and *Another Woman Who Looks Like Me* (Black Sparrow at Godine). Her website: **www.lynlifshin.com**.

A half-breed Indian, **Adrian C. Louis** was born and raised in northern Nevada and is an enrolled member of the Lovelock Paiute Tribe. From 1984-97, Louis taught at Oglala Lakota College on the Pine Ridge Reservation of South Dakota. He is currently Professor of English at the Minnesota State University in Marshall, MN. He has written ten books of poems and two works of fiction.

Deborah J. Meltvedt is a Medical Science teacher and Program Director at a small, public high school in Sacramento. She loves to blend health and medical viewpoints with creative writing, not only in her own pieces, but in the hard gripped hands of her high school students. In between writing stories, poetry, and lesson plans, Deborah loves running and traveling with her writer-husband, Rick.

April Peletta sifts through the hard and soft muck of life by pounding thoughts into word flesh. As a daughter, sister, and friend, she tries to leave the metaphors on the page or at least in her head and laugh as much as she can. She's currently studying creative writing at Mills College.

Emily Pérez's poems have appeared in journals including *Crab Orchard Review, Third Coast, Borderlands, The Laurel Review, DIAGRAM,* and *Nimrod.* Her first chapbook, *Backyard Migration Route,* is forthcoming from Finishing Line Press. She teaches English, poetry, and Gender Studies in Seattle where she lives with her husband and son.

Gordon Preston has had poems in *Blue Mesa Review, Comstock Review, Cutbank, The Missouri Review, Rattle, Tar Wolf Review,* and elsewhere. He was 54 when Finishing Line Press published his first chapbook, *Violins.* Now at 60, he still teaches reading and writing to the very young in Modesto, California.

Zara Raab's new book is *Swimming the Eel* (David Robert Books, 2011). She grew up on the rural coast of Northern California. Her poems appear in *West Branch, Crab Orchard Review, The Dark Horse, River Styx,* and elsewhere. She lives in Berkeley, CA.

Matthew Rodgers is a young poet who enjoys a receptive audience in Northern California. He is the sort of writer who brings forth both old and new forms.

Tim Sandefur is an attorney and author in Sacramento, California.

Geoff Stevens is a British poet and editor of *Purple Patch* poetry magazine since 1976. His own poetry is published regularly around the world, and his current book is *Islands In The Blood* from the U.K., publisher *Indigo Dreams*. See more at his website: **www. geoffstevens.co.uk**.

Judith Tannenbaum's most recent book is *By Heart: Poetry, Prison, and Two Lives* (with Spoon Jackson). Her other books include: *Disguised as a Poem: My Years Teaching Poetry at San Quentin,* two texts for teachers, and six poetry collections. Judith is training coordinator for WritersCorps in San Francisco. Find information about prison arts and teaching arts at **www.judithtannenbaum.com.**

Diana Thurm is an 18-year-old English major at Cosumnes River College, CA. She will be attending California State University, Sacramento in the fall, where she will be studying journalism as her major and French as her minor. Her hobbies include reading, writing, playing piano, and shopping for antiques. She began writing poetry when she was six-years old.

Ann Wehrman's writing has appeared in print and online journals including *Sacramento News & Review, Medusa's Kitchen, The Ophidian, Rattlesnake Review,* and *Poetry Now.* Ann teaches writing at American River College and online for University of Phoenix. Rattlesnake Press published her broadside, *Notes from the Ivory Tower,* in 2007 and her chapbook, *Inside (love poems),* in 2011.

Mark Wisniewski is the author of the novel *Confessions of a Polish Used Car Salesman,* the collection of short stories *All Weekend with the Lights On,* and the book of narrative poems *One of Us One Night.* His fiction has appeared in *The Southern Review, New England Review, Virginia Quarterly Review, The Yale Review,* and elsewhere. Mark's work has been anthologized in *Pushcart Prize* and *Best American Short Stories.*

About the Staff

Linda Collins, co-editor, lives and writes in Carmichael, CA. Her poetry has appeared in *American River Review, Poetry Now, Susurrus, Rattlesnake Review,* and elsewhere. She has served on the board of the Sacramento Poetry Center for four years.

Theresa McCourt, co-editor, M.A., won the 2008 Albert and Elaine Borchard Poetry Fellowship and graduated from the Artist Residency Institute via Sacramento's Metropolitan Arts Commission. Credits include *The Squaw Valley Review,* Bill Gainer's *Magnet Project,* and *Peter Parasol.* She was editor-in-chief for the Auditor General's Office (CA) and later built a seminar business. For eight years, she also wrote bi-weekly columns for *The Sacramento Bee.*

Laura Martin, graphic designer, is also a freelance writer and photographer whose work has appeared in *Via Magazine,* the *San Jose Mercury News,* the *Boston Globe,* the *San Francisco Chronicle, Sacramento Magazine, Solano Magazine, Susurrus,* and other publications throughout Northern California. She is an Amherst Writers and Artists affiliate and leads public and private writing workshops throughout the Sacramento and Davis areas.

Jane Blue, cover photographer, was born and raised in Berkeley, CA. Her poems have appeared in print and on-line magazines such as *River Oak Review, Umbrella, Stirring, The Innisfree Poetry Journal, Avatar Review, The Chattahoochee Review, Poetry International,* and others. Her most recent books are *Turf Daisies and Dandelions,* Rattlesnake Press, Sacramento, and *The Persistence of Vision,* Poets Corner Press, Stockton. She has taught creative writing at women's centers, colleges, prisons, and privately. She lives near the Sacramento River with her husband, Peter Rodman.

Notes

Made in USA (Front Porch) by Kenneth DiMaggio was previously published in the Fall 2011 issue of *The Story-teller.*

Doctor's Office, by Deborah J. Meltvedt, was previously published in the Spring, 2010 issue of *Susurrus*, Sacramento City College Literary Magazine.

"Jane," by Gordon Preston, refers to a photo by Sharon Wharton in *The Sun*, Issue #340, April 2004.

Long Shadows, by Michael Campagnoli, is included in a circulating chapbook called *The Home Stretch* and was previously published in *Illuminations* (No. 24, Summer 2008).

We Welcome Your Submissions
for the next *Tule Review*

Please read our current submission guidelines at

http://www.sacramentopoetrycenter.com/publications/the-tule-review/

Email submissions to:
tulereview@sacramentopoetrycenter.com

Mail hard copy submissions to:
Sacramento Poetry Center
1719 25th Street
Sacramento, CA 95816